Coaching the Whole Child:

Positive Development Through Sport

sports coach UK is the brand name of The National Coaching Foundation and has been such since April 2001.

ISBN: 978-1-905540-78-5

Author
David Haskins

Development Editors
Sergio Lara-Bercial
Jon Woodward

Technical Editor
Ian Stafford

Coachwise editorial and design team
Craig Smith and Matthew Dodd

Acknowledgements
Thanks to: Graham Ross for working tirelessly on the Participant Development Model and facilitating much of this material; Jean Côté for suggesting the use of the 5Cs model in the UK; Professor Richard Bailey for his early work adapting the 5Cs; and Rod Thorpe for his advice and guidance on the positioning of the 5Cs.

Throughout this resource, the term parent includes carers, guardians and other next-of-kin categories.

Cover photograph © Alan Edwards

Inner photographs © Alan Edwards unless otherwise stated.

Published on behalf of sports coach UK by:

Coachwise Business Solutions

sports coach UK
114 Cardigan Road
Headingley
Leeds LS6 3BJ

Tel: 0113-274 4802
Fax: 0113-275 5019
Email: coaching@sportscoachuk.org
Website: www.sportscoachuk.org

Patron: HRH The Princess Royal

Coachwise Business Solutions
Chelsea Close
Off Amberley Road
Armley
Leeds LS12 4HP

Tel: 0113-231 1310
Fax: 0113-231 9606
Email: enquiries@coachwisesolutions.co.uk
Website: www.coachwisesolutions.co.uk

sports coach UK will ensure that it has professional and ethical values and that all its practices are inclusive and equitable.

David Haskins is a visiting fellow in sports development at Sheffield Hallam University. He was also a reader in sports development and physical education at Liverpool John Moores University 1996–2007. David has undertaken extensive work with Youth Sport Trust (YST), editing and contributing to many of its resources. He is currently a consultant working with YST, Beckwith International Leadership Development, sports coach UK and UK Sport.

© Boswell Photographic

Foreword

In years gone by, when the question was posed about the difference between coaching and teaching, a standard response was: teachers teach children and coaches coach sport. This suggests the prevailing view that teaching was a more holistic, child-centred activity; whereas coaching concerned itself with the narrower, or more focused, activity of improving participants' sport-specific skills. In recent times, one key issue facing coach education has been whether it should be designed to produce coaches who can develop participants either **in** sport or **through** sport, or both.

Currently, the prevailing consensus appears to be that coaches, particularly those who work with children and young people, need to be developing participants not only as sports participants, but also as people. Sport is seen as an appropriate vehicle for addressing social issues such as health, challenging behaviour and community cohesion. It also appears important in its own right in terms of the intrinsic enjoyment it provides, and the sense of achievement it can instil.

There is no doubt that promoting positive youth development is a fundamentally important activity in terms of its value to individuals, communities and society. There have been many newsworthy accounts of famous participants who have attributed their experience in sport to providing them with the focus and outlet they needed to stay out of trouble and live a more fulfilling and productive life. Although it is high-level participants who tend to make the headlines, with such stories reinforcing the power of sport, the vast majority of participants who attend community clubs are just as likely to be influenced by their experiences.

The maxim in relation to influencing participants has always been: get to them early, acknowledged by the fact many adult behaviour patterns can be traced back to childhood and youth experiences. One key, constant factor in all sport, from community clubs to the Olympic and Paralympic podiums, is the coach. Coaches who work with children and young people need to acknowledge that if they really want to explore and

utilise the full power of sport, they not only have to concern themselves with improving their young participants' sports skills, but also with developing them as people who are healthy, fulfilled and prepared to become constructive members of society.

If you, as a coach, truly believe in, and are committed to, developing participants both **in** and **through** sport, you need to adopt the holistic view of what coaching entails, much like the role only formerly ascribed to teachers, and take note of what the **5Cs for coaching** approach has to offer. This approach has its roots in positive youth development and not sport. Surely, as a committed coach, you do not need to be convinced as to the potential power of sport to influence and even change lives for the better. Working with children and young people provides perhaps the greatest opportunities for shaping lives, if coaches are able to:

* identify such opportunities
* understand key principles
* have the skills to put theory into practice.

This resource should help you in all of these areas. Read, reflect, learn and apply what you have learnt. The significance and value of this resource is not in how many people read it, but how many coaches apply the key messages and the number of children and young people whose lives are changed for the better through their experiences in sport.

Ian Stafford
Writer and consultant in education and sport

Contents   Page

The 5Cs for coaching will excite all coaches of young participants, offering them the chance to reconsider the emphasis of their coaching and give them useful tools to enhance the experience of young people. The original 5Cs model (Lerner et al, 2000) was developed to enhance the positive development of young participants, and the 5Cs for coaching does exactly the same. It will enhance the development of all young participants who are being coached, by offering them an exciting, challenging and well-structured environment in which they can discover **all** that is good about sport.

The resource mentions some significant people. For those unfamiliar with these names, short biographies are included below.

Jean Côté is Professor and Director of the School of Kinesiology and Health Studies at Queen's University at Kingston in Canada. He has written many articles about the positive ways young people can become involved in sport. Unsurprisingly, he is now interested in the 5Cs and has adapted his own version.

Professor Richard Bailey was, at one time, one of the youngest professors of physical education in the UK. He is an expert on children's physical development, especially those who are gifted and talented. Richard worked with David Morley to develop the five abilities for YST.

Those of you who have heard about long-term athlete development (LTAD), Multi-skills and FUNdamentals, may not be aware these are the works of Istvan Balyi. Istvan has spent a great deal of time in the UK tutoring on his models, which have been adapted and integrated worldwide.

Rod Thorpe is one of the most influential thinkers in sport and physical education. His early applied work on Teaching Games for Understanding (TGfU) led to the publication of the TOPs resources, produced by YST. Rod's work is still being used all over the world.

SECTION ONE
The 5Cs for Coaching

Most coaches are familiar with the approach for coaching that considers the development of any participant under the following headings:

- Physical
- Mental
- Technical
- Tactical
- Personal and Social.

Coaches will place different emphasis on each of these components as appropriate; doing this offers a useful and accepted structure.

In 2008, sports coach UK commissioned a group of acknowledged experts to show how young people develop using this approach. The group included Professor Richard Bailey, Istvan Balyi, Clive Brewer, Dave Collins, Jean Côté, Pat Duffy and Rod Thorpe. The following table gives a summary of their suggested appropriate development for 8–12 year olds.

Table 1: Suggested development for 8–12 year olds in key physical, mental, technical and tactical aspects of sport

Physical	Mental	Technical	Tactical
Children should be:			
• confident and competent with basic agility, balance and coordination	• confident when active and demonstrate a commitment to improving	• modifying basic skills to meet specific needs and broadening their skill base	• performing in modified sports with modified rules
• learning about speed and its uses, and practising how to gain speed in different ways and reduce speed and stop safely	• setting simple goals and beginning to use self-talk	• showing quality with specific techniques/skills	• showing a basic understanding of force, space and time to develop more sophisticated tactics
• able to demonstrate a range of movement and mobility	• able to combine basic skills efficiently • scanning and making dynamic decisions based on information • mastering object control in different environments	• getting into a routine of practice as frequently as appropriate and necessary	• shaping their technical work to match the tactical challenge
• beginning to use strength and power, and developing endurance	• using others' strengths when performing with them and showing task orientation	• introduced to appropriate competition	• refining attention to sensory input.

Looking at Table 1, the importance of each component is clear. You will be able to see that each has a valuable role in the development of young participants.

Using Table 1, think about how you could develop physical, mental, technical and tactical components. The following questions might help:

Physical

How do I help young participants develop general movement expertise and not just that which is useful for my sport?

Mental

How do I help young participants begin to make decisions and influence performance with their thinking?

Technical

How do I prepare young participants to develop specific skills?

Tactical

How do I help young participants understand their sport and how they can influence the way it is played or performed?

Personal and social development has been omitted from Table 1 because this resource explains a new approach to this key aspect of development. Personal and social development has great significance, especially when coaching young participants. For many young participants, involvement in sport is a fundamental part of their personal and social development. It is not simply part of their involvement with sport; it becomes part of them.

An excellent model for describing the personal and social development of young participants is being used within youth development. It is called the 5Cs for positive youth development.

The 5Cs are:

- competence
- confidence
- connection
- character
- caring (Lerner et al, 2000).

The simplified definitions of these terms can be found in Table 2.

Table 2: Definitions of the 5Cs (extended and adapted from Roth and Brooks-Gunn, 2003)

Competence:	Positive view of one's actions with appropriate capability
Confidence:	An internal sense of overall positive self-worth and being good at things
Connection:	Positive bonds with people and institutions
Character:	Respect for societal and cultural rules, possession of standards for correct behaviours, a sense of right and wrong, and integrity
Caring:	A sense of sympathy and empathy for others.

As the model was proposed and discussed for use in coaching, some adaptations were made. Firstly, it was suggested **creativity** was another important 'C'. This fitted well with the work of Rod Thorpe on TGfU (Bunker and Thorpe, 1982) and Games Sense, where participants were helped to find their own solutions to problems by being encouraged to work creatively. Professor Richard Bailey and David Morley (2006) had also included creativity as one of the five abilities for gifted and talented athletes. Côté and Gilbert (2009) also carried out work on the 5Cs model and suggested combining character and caring. It was from this that the 5Cs for coaching emerged, and this is the model used throughout this resource.

Jean Côté is fully committed to this model and has written a useful paper (Côté et al, in press) that gives a full justification of the use of the 5Cs within the coaching field. What's more, Côté offered full significance to the model when he proposed the following definition of coaching expertise:

Consistent application of sport-specific, interpersonal and intrapersonal knowledge to improve athletes' competence, confidence, connection and character in a specific coaching context.

Jean Côté

Table 3: Adaptation of the 5Cs for use in sports coaching

Competence:	Positive view of one's actions with appropriate capability
Confidence:	An internal sense of overall positive self-worth and being good at things
Connection:	Positive bonds with people and institutions
Character and Caring:	Respect for societal and cultural rules, possession of standards for correct behaviours, a sense of right and wrong, and a sense of sympathy and empathy for others
Creativity:	Finding one's own solutions.

SECTION TWO
Fitting Together the New and the Accepted

Côté's definition from the previous section really does integrate the 5Cs for coaching with our accepted model of development for participants. What is being suggested is that whenever participants learn anything, their personal and social development will affect the way they learn.

In diagrammatic form, using the original model looks like this:

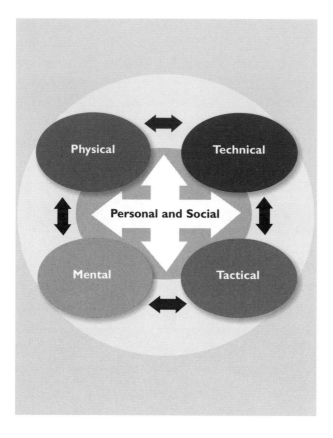

Figure 1: The physical, mental, technical, tactical, and personal and social model

The introduction of the 5Cs adds more detail to the model and begins to show, quite clearly, why the 5Cs are important, as each of them interacts with the other four parts of physical, mental, technical and tactical development.

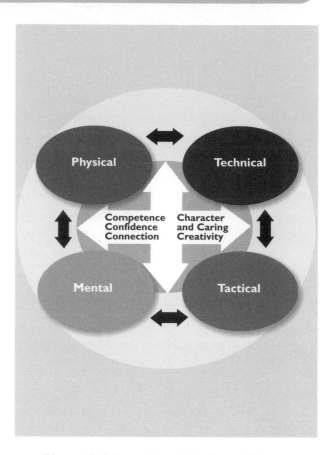

Figure 2: Adapted model of coaching to show the position of the 5Cs

It is easy to see how competence, confidence and creativity affect the way the physical, technical and tactical aspects of any sport are learnt by a participant. These aspects are crucial. As our understanding of the 5Cs increases, it will also become apparent how much the connection and character aspects add to the sporting experience, the development of participants, and to the overall development of sport.

Many coaches will discover the 5Cs framework simply gives them a structure for integrating their already excellent practice, and provides a sound justification for what they have been doing for years. The advantage of having a structure is that it will allow us to add knowledge to specific areas and not just integrate current practice, but develop even better practice.

Table 4 offers a start to the structure, showing how coaches could begin to incorporate a 5Cs environment for their coaching.

Table 4: How the 5Cs could be included in coaching programmes

	Participants should:
Competence:	• be in a coaching environment where appropriate techniques and skills are learnt in a progressive and enjoyable way
Confidence:	• enjoy success when practising and receive positive and beneficial feedback
Connection:	• work by themselves and in groups so they enjoy the benefits of team play • work with others and eventually enjoy the independence of community sport • understand and state the benefits of exercise, and when and where it can be accessed appropriately
Character and Caring:	• practise in an environment that respects players, coaches, officials and the rules of all sports
Creativity:	• be encouraged to find their own solutions to problems so they learn and understand, rather than simply copying and repeating.

There are more issues arising from Table 4 than might be thought of at first glance. Careful consideration should indicate there are elements all of us acknowledge as important, but that aren't always integrated within our coaching practice.

Of course, within all this, there is another very important element – you, the coach. The actual practice of the coach will affect the way the 5Cs are included and delivered. Reflecting on your own coaching practice will be a very important element of including the 5Cs and the impact they have on young participants.

Below is a simple reflective checklist for you to try.

Table 5: Reflective activity 1

Could You...	Now or Soon?	How Will I Do It? (make your own notes here)
• encourage young participants to reflect on their performance during sessions, allowing both of you to gain a good idea of competence		
• give accurate, informative and positive feedback to young participants to build their confidence		
• adopt a team approach to almost everything you do to encourage connection		
• ensure your practice and the performance of young participants is always underpinned by a code of good, ethical practice to build character		
• encourage problem solving whenever possible to build creativity?		

After reading these first two chapters, we hope you are getting excited about the 5Cs for coaching model; not just because it is new, but because it really gives us a way of improving participants and fully integrating them with the sports we all love.

Before we delve deeper into the principles of the 5Cs model, it is worth, at this point, explaining the Participant Development Model. As a result of the important work of Balyi and Côté, a model has been devised that shows how everyone can start and stay involved in sport.

Follow Figure 3 (below) by starting with Active Start, and then through the next two stages of FUNdamentals and Learning to Play and Practice (these are the stages with which this resource is concerned). After this, the model begins to specialise, with elite participants moving to the right, and those that play sport for enjoyment and, hopefully, for the rest of their lives, moving to the left. Use the model to identify where you do most of your coaching.

The following chapters explain the 5Cs in more detail.

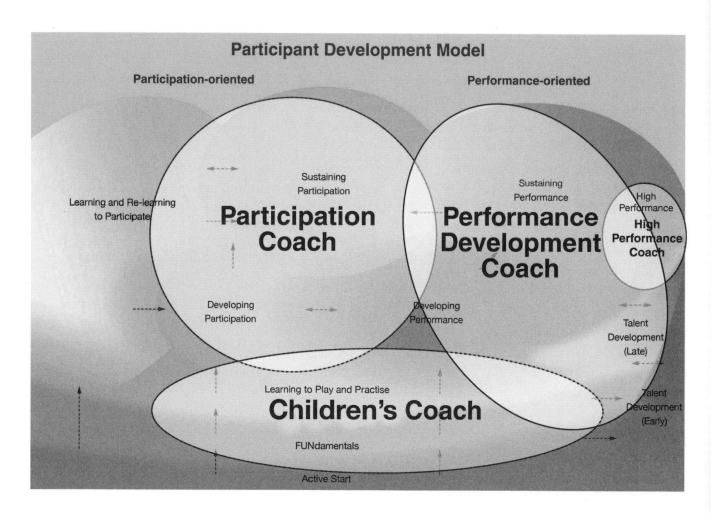

Figure 3: Participant Development Model

SECTION THREE
Competence

To achieve **competence**, participants should obtain a positive view of their own actions by being in a coaching environment where appropriate techniques and skills are learnt in a progressive and enjoyable way.

After a certain stage, as young participants begin to specialise, the development of competence in a particular sport is determined to a great extent by the governing body of sport. Courses at Level 1 and 2 prepare coaches for specific work in their sport and focus on the development of specific capability.

It is important for coaches to consider those participants who choose to take up sport not for the pursuit of excellence, but simply for recreation or health reasons.

The stages before specialisation, as young participants prepare for an active life in sport, are perhaps the most important. This early development can provide the perfect foundation for later progression.

Balyi's work in devising the LTAD model has enhanced our understanding of key developmental issues and stages young participants experience. Many coaches are familiar with including and emphasising the ABCs (agility, balance, coordination and speed) and Multi-skills activities in their sessions.

The current Participant Development Model with which many sports are operating, and that is based on Balyi's work, lists three early stages for young people. The stages are now advocated across the UK and form part of The UK Coaching Framework. These stages are:

- Active Start
- FUNdamentals
- Learning to Play and Practice.

Active Start (up to approximately six years of age)

Active Start is the stage aimed at developing rudimentary movement, early fundamental movement skills, and a love and enjoyment of physical activity. At this stage, children should be provided with informal learning opportunities in home and pre-school environments. Success for children at this stage can be defined as playing with confidence, while learning and developing competence in fundamental movement skills in an appropriate and stimulating environment.

Table 6 suggests appropriate development during this important stage.

Table 6: Active Start – suggested development of key aspects

Physical	Mental	Technical	Tactical
Children should be:			
• developing balance and stability through simple gymnastic, dance and other movement activities	• becoming self-aware and beginning to think about, and reflect on, performance	• developing basic general movement skills	• responding to the environment
• playing with, and controlling, objects	• developing basic skills	• practising sending (throwing) and receiving (catching) objects	• watching others
• travelling in different ways by changing speed and level	• playing collaboratively by being aware of, and using, others	• observing and copying others	• understanding object movement and space.

With this group of young participants, coaches, parents and leaders should be developing competence by:

- providing balance, coordination and general movement experiences

- providing experiences that enable children to respond to varied environments

- allowing children to play in informal and less-structured environments

- working with small groups of children

- including all children in play

- offering children the chance to practise and be successful

- building confidence

- encouraging children to play with others and respond appropriately

- talking to children about their experiences

- beginning to structure some experiences

- helping children understand the benefits of exercise and eating and drinking properly

- developing performance through festivals and celebrations of skill.

© The Gymnastics Factory

What a great list and what fun and enjoyment these young participants could have if all coaches provided this type of experience. Here is an example from a gymnastics club in Guildford.

The Gymnastics Factory in Guildford, run by Sine Rance, claims to build happy, healthy children, and the sign on the door says 'smile before you enter'. There is every reason to smile because of the quality of what is on offer.

The gym-bug classes, for children aged four months to five years, are specifically designed to focus on all the basic movement skills through developing balance, coordination, strength, agility, speed, body and spatial awareness. Children use an extensive range of specialised equipment in what is an excellent programme of all-round physical development.

During the programmes, children will be encouraged to use:

- footballs and goals

- plastic golf equipment

- foam tennis balls for rolling and bowling

- hoops, balls, beanbags of different shapes, and quoits

- scarves and ribbon sticks

- pegs for fine manipulation.

Activity stations are also set up, with specifically designed themes that include:

- running and jumping into a pit

- developing coordination by putting quoits on cones, beanbags on spots, doing manipulative puzzles, posting cards in boxes, and playing hopscotch

- swinging off tiny parallel bars, suspending from bars and manipulating hanging objects

- using benches, beams and ramps to develop movement capabilities, along with having opportunities to step and jump over obstacles.

The Gymnastics Factory is the perfect example where focus on all-round development leads to satisfying movement and developmental experiences for children. It is clear the activities help to develop every aspect of the 5Cs, as well as offering appropriate physical, technical, tactical and mental development.

FUNdamentals (approximately 6-9 years of age)

At this stage, focus is on the development of a broad range of fundamental skills in a playful context. Success for children at this stage can be defined as building competence and confidence through the learning of fundamental movement skills.

This involves the provision of positive learning environments both in and out of school settings, to develop a broad range of fundamental skills within a fun and playful context. As these key underpinning skills build basic competence and confidence, they play an important part in contributing to participation in sport and developing more advanced skills in later years. Table 7 suggests appropriate development during this important stage.

Table 7: FUNdamentals – suggested development of key aspects

Physical	Mental	Technical	Tactical
Children should be:			
• developing foundation movement qualities by further exposure to activities involving agility, balance and coordination	• reflecting on performance correctly and showing self-reinforcement and determination	• developing and refining basic movement skills and applying them to sport-specific activity	• able to focus senses and perception
• travelling at different levels in different ways	• able to refocus after a distraction • planning simple activities	• using a variety of equipment	• able to understand the essential requirements of an activity challenge
• controlling objects on both sides of the body, and beginning to use both hands and feet competently	• using a combination of skills • making decisions	• able to understand the criteria for performance in certain sports (eg gymnastics)	• aware of the concepts of space, time and possession.
	• differentiating between team and individual performance		

When working with young participants at this stage, coaches should be developing competence by:

- building physical competence in balance, coordination and movement in a Multi-skills environment
- providing experiences to enable children to respond to varied environments, including other children's movements
- allowing children to play freely within safe limits
- offering some children special help to enable them to play
- working with small groups of children
- offering children the chance to practise, be successful, and to make changes to practices
- building confidence

- structuring activities so children have to cooperate with others and respond appropriately
- encouraging children to talk and think about their experiences
- structuring experiences that lead to sport-specific skills
- helping children to learn some simple rules of activities
- getting children to talk about the benefits of exercise, and eating and drinking properly
- helping young participants take advantage of the Five Hour Offer that is part of current government strategy
- developing performance through simple competitive situations, including Multi-skills festivals.

Hessle Rangers in Hull (right) are operating a Football FUNdamentals programme called 1st Touch Football at Sirius Academy. The Saturday morning club consists of two, one-hour sessions for 5–6 year olds and 7–8 year olds. There are also plans to run courses in feeder schools and in the holidays.

The advertised principles of the programme are to:

- encourage children to be creative and try new ideas and be comfortable on the ball
- emphasise fun and enjoyment as the most important tools in a young child's learning
- learn through succeeding and failing, as making mistakes helps children improve (eg 'we encourage children to help us set up some of our practices and then explore what possibilities can be achieved')
- ask the children open-ended questions to help them understand the problem and improve (eg 'what made you try and go for that target?')
- help children go out there and give it a go!

The 1st Touch Football programme at Hessle Rangers encourages children to be comfortable, creative and to enjoy playing football. The club also states its programme helps to develop:

- ABCs, as well as posture
- cognitive skills
- self-confidence and social skills
- body awareness and understanding of the benefits of exercise.

This programme is a very good example of the integration of the 5Cs and physical, technical, tactical and mental development. The club articulates clearly how it will build competence, confidence, connection, character and creativity through structured and developmental practices. Further connection is gained from the fact young participants are encouraged to join Hessle Rangers to take part in its Mini-Soccer programme.

The Football Association (FA) is in a very strong position to help clubs like Hessle Rangers, as it has a specific child coach award.

Frodsham Athletics Club is fortunate to have George Bunner MBE as founder and coach. George has developed many innovative approaches to athletics and has recently developed an Infant Agility Challenge for the young participants at the club, and for a wider audience through Eveque Leisure Equipment Ltd. Examples of the activites include:

- pitcher – throwing beanbags at a target
- striker – kicking a ball at targets
- stepper – a simple hurdle/stepping activity
- bowler – rolling a ball at a target
- launcher – two-handed throw at a wall
- thrower – one-handed throw of a soft javelin
- jumper – a two-footed standing jump.

The activities are simple and rewarding, and could be used by any coach to help young participants at this stage.

Learning to Play and Practice (approximately 8-12 years of age)

The emphasis during this stage is on sampling a range of sports, developing basic sports skills, and continuing to build children's competence and confidence. This is achieved by the application of fundamental movement skills, while learning the skills required for different sports. The main features of this stage are the provision of appropriate opportunities for participants to learn to play and practice a wide range of different sports, activities and skills in the later years of primary school.

Table 8: Learning to Play and Practice – suggested development of key aspects

Physical	Mental	Technical	Tactical
Children should be:			
• confident and competent with basic agility, balance and coordination	• confident when active, showing a commitment to improve	• modifying basic skills to meet specific needs and broadening their skill base	• performing in modified sports with modified rules
• learning about speed and its uses, practising how to gain speed in different ways, and how to slow down and stop with control	• setting simple goals and beginning to use self-talk	• showing quality with specific techniques/skills	• showing a basic understanding of force, space and time, to develop more sophisticated tactics
• able to demonstrate a range of movement and mobility	• able to combine basic skills efficiently • scanning and making decisions based on information • mastering object control in different environments	• getting into a routine of practice as frequently as appropriate and necessary	• shaping their technical work to match the tactical challenge
• beginning to use strength and power, and developing endurance	• using others' strengths when performing with them and showing task orientation	• introduced to appropriate competition	• refining attention to sensory input.

With this group of young participants, coaches should be developing competence by:

• transferring physical competence in balance, coordination and movement into sport-specific activities

• using these skills and those related to perception and decision making to solve sport-based challenges

• building on good practice in high-quality physical education

• allowing children to sample a broad and balanced variety of sports in different sporting environments

• giving children access to Multi-skills clubs and academies

• working with small groups of children

• offering children the chance to practise, be successful, and to make changes to practices

• ensuring all children are able to approach activities with confidence, by adapting practices for some children to maximise their chances of achievement

• structuring activities so children have to work in teams and respond appropriately

• encouraging children to talk about, reflect and suggest improvements to their performance that are then tried out in practice

• helping children to use sport-specific skills in appropriate activities

• progressing performance through appropriate competitions from the national competition framework, ensuring the ratio of competition to practice does not exceed 30:70.

Oliver Waldram is 12 years old and a keen member of the Basingstoke Bluefins, where he plays water polo and swims to a high standard. As well as physical education and school sport, where Oliver plays hockey, he is involved in an extensive training programme with his club. Oliver practices water polo one night a week and also takes part in swimming and dry-land sessions. He has played water polo in the London league and at the Hampshire Mini Games, won six gold medals at the club's new year meet, and finished sixth overall in the Hampshire County Championships. Oliver is a good example of a young person learning to play and practice. Even in a sport as challenging as swimming, his club and parents are helping him develop, by offering different sports to practise and in which to take part.

Introduced to appropriate competition

Showing quality with specific techniques and skills

Take another look at the profile of Oliver. Then look at Table 8 on the previous page and consider how much his involvement in sport is contributing to the different key aspects.

SECTION FOUR
Confidence

Confidence in all participants can affect:

*   joining in
*   being able to perform well
*   gaining maximum benefit from participation
*   opting out
*   underperforming
*   having negative experiences in sport.

How many times have you, as a coach, said: 'they seem to have lost confidence'? The phrase itself is interesting, as it implies confidence is a quality you either have or do not have. Of course, this isn't true and coaches have a responsibility to help participants develop and gain confidence as they practise.

The 5Cs defines confidence as an internal sense of overall positive self-worth and self-efficacy.

The 5Cs for coaching states participants should enjoy success when practising and receive positive and beneficial feedback.

It is worth examining all the key words in the definitions to see how they should affect your coaching practice.

Self-worth

Many participants take part in sport because they want to. Sport is important to them because it is something they are good at, and they enjoy that feeling. It is the responsibility of coaches to use and build this sense of self-worth. Sport has much to offer in the development of self-worth, such as:

*   feeling a sense of accomplishment when winning
*   knowing you tried your best when losing
*   practising repeatedly to improve
*   making a great pass for someone else to score
*   running or swimming a great relay leg.

The list is endless and we have to acknowledge how many opportunities there are.

Self-efficacy

Self-efficacy can be simply explained as knowing and believing you can do something. It is considered one of the main factors for young participants either continuing or giving up sport. One disturbing finding from the Nike Girls in Sport project (Youth Sport Trust, 2007) showed many teenage girls did not lose capability, but lost the belief they had it. The coach's role in building self-efficacy is twofold. Firstly, the coach has to help build the skills participants need, before helping them realise they really do possess the skills and can use them. It is important to realise players having skills and believing they have skills are not the same thing.

Before considering the idea of success in practices and positive feedback, let's take a look at the development of confidence in the 5Cs for coaching.

Table 9: The phased development of confidence in the 5Cs for coaching

Stage	Examples of Key Aspects Related to Confidence
Active Start	<ul><li>Developing psychologically in different play environments by becoming aware of their own ability and being encouraged to feel good about their performance</li><li>Showing satisfaction in their achievements and improvement</li><li>At least 80% successful through the careful provision of differentiated activities</li></ul>
FUNdamentals	<ul><li>Developing psychologically in more structured activities by showing optimistic perceptions of their own physical ability</li><li>Taking responsibility for their achievements and improvement</li><li>At least 80% successful through the careful provision of differentiated activities</li></ul>
Learning to Play and Practice	<ul><li>Talking with pride about their achievements and improvements</li><li>Being responsive, attentive and actively engaged in physical activities.</li></ul>

Two features stand out within the development of confidence. Firstly, the responsibility of coaches to allow participants to be successful, and, secondly, that emerging participants need to feel good about performance and begin to understand what good performance is. Let's take a look at what coaches could do.

Enjoying Success when Practising – Using Differentiation

Teachers are used to the idea of differentiation. This is the practice of giving each child an appropriate task tailored to their individual needs. Teachers achieve differentiation with careful planning, structured activities, and by providing additional support, as well as concise record keeping.

Coaches also need to differentiate, and, for some, it is accepted practice. Attackers and defenders may do different things; players may practise different moves; runners will train for different events. The idea of differentiation can go further, and success in practice is important here.

If a coach sets the same task for a group of 15 participants, at what level does she aim: the top, middle or lower level? It is a difficult task. By dividing a group of 15 into three groups of five, or even five groups of three, based on similarity of need, the task becomes much less difficult. In a small group, with an appropriate task, participants can be challenged appropriately so they achieve a good level of success. If the coach teaches players how to change the task, they are then able to adjust it themselves, leaving the coach free to give feedback.

When using differentiation, care needs to be taken to avoid making assumptions and not always using the same groups for all activities. Coaches can always try mixed ability groupings to ensure participants get the chance to demonstrate improvement and reap the benefits of performing with participants of varied skill levels. This may lead to enhanced collaborative skills, cooperation and increased performance for some, thus helping participants develop as people and become more effective in the sporting environment.

STEP

A powerful tool for differentiation is the STEP model, used on many of the TOPs cards produced by YST. The STEP model gives advice on how to change the

Space

Task

Equipment

People

for any activity.

The below example, set out by Howard Todd on the TOPs gymnastic cards (Youth Sport Trust, 2003), shows how STEP can be used with the simple task of travelling, using hands and feet.

Easier

S – travel forwards in a straight line

T – show two ways of travelling, using combinations of hands and feet

E – move forwards along a bench using a simple walk

P – play 'follow the leader' in pairs.

Harder

S – travel around the perimeter of a square or rectangular area, using different steps on each side and linked smoothly at the corners

T – chassé step with change of leg, performed backwards and to the side

E – perform combinations of travelling steps on a low beam; devise a short travelling routine with a partner, where you match the dance links

P – make a travelling routine with another person.

Positive and Beneficial Feedback

All participants like to receive positive feedback. This has been referred to as 'catching someone out being good'. Players will learn from, and respond to, positive feedback, and it also tends to set the tone for participant interaction and communication.

Positive feedback becomes more beneficial when it gives participants precise information about what exactly was good. The phrases: 'that was great', 'super', 'excellent' and 'fantastic', are all examples of positive feedback. But where is the specific technical feedback?

It is worth considering these statements:

'The way you changed pace in the last five metres was excellent.'

'What a great clearance from defence, they were all over our right side and you passed the ball wide left.'

Of course, the above statements could be accompanied by a question or confirmation, which would lead to more feedback.

Statement of Beneficial Feedback	Question or Confirmation
The way you changed pace in the last five metres was excellent.	How did you know the other runner was so close? Or, I think it is because you have worked so hard at strength training.
What a great clearance from defence, they were all over our right side and you passed the ball wide left.	How can we make passes to the left even better? Or, ...and you passed the ball at just the right pace.

More About Confidence

The study of confidence in sport is a subject in itself. Those wishing to delve further into the subject could consult the following reference:

Fuller, N., Chapman, J. and Jolly, S. (2009) *Positive Behaviour Management in Sport*. Leeds: Coachwise Business Solutions. ISBN: 978-1-905540-58-7, pp. 3–7.

SECTION FIVE
Connection

The initial explanation of **connection** is: positive bonds with people and institutions.

All coaches understand the power and importance of sport in helping to foster and develop positive bonds. Initially, young people start by playing with someone else, probably a parent, before gradually making progress through playing with another and playing in groups, before being a member of a squad or team.

It is easy to see connection as one of the benefits of being involved in physical activity, but it is also important to realise it is something coaches can affect with their practice. Actions such as moving to small group play at the right time, making someone a captain when it is just the thing they need, including someone in a squad when they thought they would be left out, and encouraging someone to learn to be an official, are all examples of when coaches can intervene to help participants make a positive connection with others and with sport. In fact, everything coaches do can help participants connect. An earlier definition stated coaches could encourage connection by allowing participants to work by themselves to enjoy the independence of community sport and, in groups, to enjoy the benefits of team play. What's more, coaches could understand and state the benefits of exercise, and when and where it can be accessed appropriately.

Some simple progressions in connection are shown in Table 10.

Table 10: The phased development of connection in the 5Cs for coaching

Stage	Young participants should:
Active Start	• respond positively to guidance and new experiences by fully participating in a variety of activities that offer opportunities for learning • begin to play with, and cooperate with, others • go with parents to outside clubs (eg toddler groups, swim and gym clubs) • begin to state the benefits of exercise
FUNdamentals	• demonstrate empathy, sensitivity and friendship skills • regularly engage in physical play, with different social groups of different sizes (eg simple games of 2 v 2 or 3 v 3) • choose independently to join out-of-school-hours clubs • go with parents to external clubs and begin to take roles in teams and squads • explain the benefits of regular exercise and how it can be undertaken safely
Learning to Play and Practice	• enjoy making friends in sporting contexts • regularly and punctually attend organised activities and care about the club, coaches and fellow players • begin to lead activities with younger children • take exercise because they fully recognise its benefits.

As you look through Table 10, you can see three themes emerging. These are:

- working with others
- helping others
- connecting with sport.

Working with Others

As soon as young children move from their initial individual play, they are capable of working with others. Coaches working with very young participants will be aware of this and begin this development slowly and appropriately. Young participants will work in pairs, threes and fours, with an emphasis on cooperation and working together on a task. As young participants progress, groupings become more complex, involving eight, 10 or 12 participants. It is at this point team games can be introduced, with cooperation in a team and competition against another team. This simple progression in team play offers a wealth of development for young participants learning about developing relationships with others.

A sample progression could look like this:

• solitary play
• co-active work, where children work alongside each other
• cooperating with another
• cooperating in groups of threes and fours
• 1 v 1 competition
• 3 v 1 and 5 v 3 to give larger groups greater success
• 2 v 1, 2 v 2, 3 v 2 and 3 v 3 competition
• progress through cooperative and competitive team play with 4 v 4, 5 v 5, 6 v 6, etc.

The following detail the important connections throughout this activity:

- cooperating
- competing
- roles in teams.

Cooperating

As young participants cooperate, they begin to learn important skills for sport. Firstly, they start to understand just what is required to make performance easier for another. For example, the ball sent to the correct place, the perfect support for a gymnastic position, the perfect baton change; all of which require the development of skill and understanding of its application. Of course, while this is happening, relationships are being built through the appreciation of the perfect pass; the smile after the perfect handstand; and the high five after winning a relay. All these actions and behaviours enable participants to appreciate others and show their appreciation.

Competing

Much has been written about the effects of competition. As far as connection is concerned, competition allows participants to begin to learn how to try to win when playing against others, while remaining on friendly terms and appreciating their good play. Competition allows a great deal of connection with the true essence of sport. Preparation, practice and performance is a cycle that is repeated frequently.

Roles in Teams

Being able to play a specific role, and play it well, is one of the fundamental requirements of teamwork. In sport, players learn the various skills required for certain positions and also begin to appreciate the skill and understanding of others as they fulfil their roles. This allows for full appreciation of the whole team and offers the individual the chance of developing real connection with others, while fulfilling a worthwhile role themselves.

Could This Be You?

- Always find time for cooperative practice and establish a habit among participants of appreciating others' good performance.

- Always encourage competitive situations, promoting the fair-play side of competition as well as the spirit of the sport, by shaking hands after a game and by positively evaluating the performance of other teams as well as your own.

- Allow participants to experience different roles and to talk with each other regarding their discoveries about themselves and others.

- Try to give different participants the role of captain and share other key responsibilities to gauge responses.

Helping Others – Leading and Coaching

At school, many young participants are expected to analyse performance. By being asked to select and apply skills, and then evaluate and improve performance, they are expected to coach themselves. By 16, the completion age for GCSEs, most young participants could be equipped to:

- choreograph a dance routine

- compose a gymnastics sequence involving changes of level and speed, using floor and apparatus

- explore the tactics of a 400m race

- evaluate the body position and breathing of someone swimming front crawl

- try to improve a time in an orienteering course

- investigate attacking options in an invasion game.

In addition to school, there are also specific programmes designed to qualify young people for leading and coaching. Sports Leaders UK (SLUK) has a range of leadership programmes that start with children as young as nine years old, with the Young Leaders Award. The familiar Junior Sports Leaders Award (JSLA) and Community Sports Leaders Award (CSLA) have been replaced with SLUK Level 1, 2 and 3 awards respectively. With the addition of governing body of sport 'bolt on'

awards, SLUK provides an excellent range of programmes to prepare young people for leadership and coaching.

Schools are realising young leaders begin to acquire skills that enable them to help others. One school in West Yorkshire (Ripponden Dene) invites 10–11 year olds to apply for jobs as playground leaders. The young people apply, are interviewed, and, if successful, receive training to enable them to lead activities in the playground. Halton (a borough of Merseyside), and many other areas in the country, run similar programmes.

The YST has been running the highly successful Step into Sport (SiS) programme. The programme operates in three stages:

- Step On (11–14 years)

- Step In (14–16 years)

- Step Out (16–19 years).

Within these stages, three principles are applied. These are:

- growing and deploying young people

- young people actively volunteering in a variety of different settings

- building a pathway leading to specific lifelong volunteering roles and potential career pathways.

Growing and Deploying Young People

This involves giving young people the skills and competencies to become leaders and volunteers. The young people are then deployed to ensure they become active leaders and volunteers, putting qualifications and training to use.

Young People Actively Volunteering in a Variety of Different Settings

This uses a twofold approach with young people who become leaders and volunteers through school, moving into volunteering in the community. Young people who already participate in community sport undertake leadership and volunteering roles in their clubs and organisations from 11 years of age.

Building a Pathway Leading to Specific Lifelong Volunteering Roles and Potential Career Pathways

This principle aims to engage young people in the range of roles necessary for the successful running of sport.

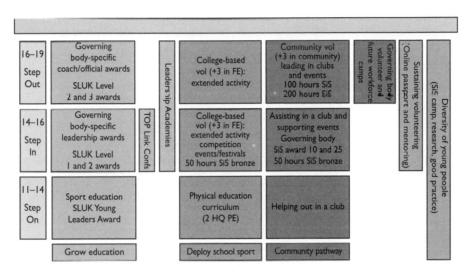

Figure 4: The Step into Sport programme

Figure 4, showing the range of activities in SiS, has most impact on clubs and coaching in the community pathway. Here, young people move from school to club with the confidence to apply their skills. As can be seen from the diagram, governing bodies of sport recognise the value of young leaders. In addition, the SiS passport scheme allows young participants to record their work in the community, where a trained mentor supports them in their new role.

All of this work is helping young participants build a valuable connection with sport through being trained to help others, and being actively encouraged to do so.

Could This Be You?

- Find out which young people in your club are on the SiS pathway.

- Discuss with young leaders how they want to develop and give them appropriate opportunities in the club.

- Develop a leader or young coach of the year award.

- Offer young leaders reduced subscriptions or other meaningful incentives.

Connecting with Sport

One of the consistent features of the national curriculum for physical education has been knowledge and understanding of fitness and health. Among the areas it covers are the effects of exercise and how children can access appropriate exercise for themselves. These are also relevant areas for coaches. From a very early age, young people can be expected to perform exercises, be involved in activity, and understand why.

One of the easiest examples is helping young people warm up. Some coaches may show young people exercises and ask them to copy, offering helpful advice on how to perform them properly. The next progression could be a simple explanation of what to do before stretching and why. Another progression could be explaining the muscles being stretched and why. All this is building a connection with sport and giving young people the information and knowledge they need to become independent and educated participants.

This simple example can be followed with all participants. It depends on coaches helping participants acquire and develop knowledge, so they can:

- understand what is happening in practices and why

- begin to plan their own progress

- understand more about their own sport, including strategy, tactics, rules, etc.

Much has been written about the responsibilities of the coach in delivering training sessions. Coaches could spend years working out what to do for their athletes, but where do athletes read about their responsibilities? Most learn about their responsibilities, in relation to training, from coaches themselves. Thus, coaches have a dual role: educating participants about the training process, and providing advice and guidance about training itself.

Consideration of three simple phases in training leads to some interesting areas of discussion.

Preparing for Training

Coaches have the ability to plan for the long- and short-term, producing constructive and progressive training sessions. The benefit of involving participants in planning is to develop their understanding of what they are supposed to be doing when training. This leads to an ability to work hard and rest appropriately, because athletes really do understand the training process. Involving participants in making decisions about, and planning, their training allows them to begin to take greater responsibility for their own development; it should also improve their level of commitment. Some interesting differences exist between the sexes. The Nike Girls in Sport and Norwich Union Girls Active projects (Youth Sport Trust, 2007) both found that intellectual engagement by girls enhances their involvement in physical activity. If they know what they are doing and understand the outcomes, they are much more able to achieve them.

Connection for participants at this stage could involve:

- practising writing and adjusting goals
- understanding long- and short-term goals
- understanding cycles of training and the physiological effects.

The Training Session

During the training session, the participant and coach work on achieving goals that have been set. Once again, if these goals are truly shared, then both athlete and coach understand what is required. The athlete, who is responding to a series of instructions, is denied real engagement with the process. Feedback, of course, should be constructive, goal orientated and educative. If goals are being achieved, coaches should tell participants precisely why, in language that will help them evaluate themselves in the future.

Connection for participants at this stage could involve:

- a joint discussion about how the athlete feels before the session
- agreement on the goals of the session before it starts
- agreed minimum and maximum output.

Evaluating and Following Up Training Sessions

With intensive schedules, it may not be possible or even necessary to evaluate every session. Coaches should always start any joint evaluation session by asking the participants themselves for their comments, views and observations. Their success at being able to lead the evaluation session will depend on the coach's ability to give them the language, knowledge, confidence and ownership, so they really feel this part of the session is theirs to lead. Coaches should then pick up on information and again use it as part of the education process, taking the participants forward so they understand the next steps.

Connection for participants at this stage could involve:

- a joint discussion of how the goals were achieved
- careful examination of the views of the athlete
- joint adjustment of goals.

© Somerset Activity and Sports Partnership

Connecting with Families

To conclude this section, it is worth considering a hugely successful aquatics scheme in Somerset, coordinated by Colin Christmas for Somerset Activity and Sports Partnership and Alison Usher, Swimming Regional Development Manager. The scheme involves the whole family in the teaching of swimming to toddlers.

It is often the child's first aquatic experience and encourages different generations to participate because of the friendly atmosphere and structured pathway. The scheme provides pre-natal aqua aerobics during the session, mother-and-baby support to toddlers and, then, after the session, an over-50s aqua aerobics session that many grandparents attend.

The project removes some of the barriers parents face in general aquatics sessions, such as having relaxed ratios as a result of in-the-water support and during changing, and swimmers being allowed to wear additional clothing in the pool.

Support staff are instrumental in the scheme's success, with trained staff on-hand to support in the water to ensure the whole experience is a positive one.

The scheme has impacted on many areas, increasing attendance at other leisure groups, such as pre-school gym and learn to swim lessons. It has also resulted in increased participation at weekends.

Swimming coaches and teachers have had to learn a new way of working. Here are some interesting comments from two of the teachers: Jackie and Laura.

'For the first six weeks, we were out of our comfort zone, although we enjoyed it. We love the programme and wouldn't want to work any other way now', said Jackie and Laura.

'It's not teaching in the usual way. We work with the adults to enable them to teach their own children. We're there to give them the confidence as well as the skills to support their own child's learning, and to develop their water confidence and movement skills in the water.'

They continued: 'One thing is that it has helped me improve and develop as a teacher. I can now focus better on the needs of each individual child in my classes and I'm better able to come up with what I need to do to help them improve and succeed.'

SECTION SIX
Character and Caring

From the time it was first played, sport has been described as something that can help build character. The definition of character within the 5Cs is:

respect for societal and cultural rules, possession of standards for correct behaviours, a sense of right and wrong, and a sense of sympathy and empathy for others.

The 5Cs for coaching states that all involved should:

practise in an environment that respects players, coaches and officials, and the rules and traditions of all sports.

The idea of **character and caring** is very similar to connection. We all assume players will develop character in sport, but, as coaches, we are often not told how to develop it deliberately and how we can include it in our practice. Try this quick self-test below.

Table 11: Reflection activity 2

Question	Yes or No?
• Do you have a code of conduct for coaches, officials and players?	
• Do you have a code of conduct for parents?	
• Do you teach your players how to thank opponents after a game?	
• Do you teach your players how to talk with each other after a game?	

• Have you ever questioned an official:
  – during a competition
  – after a competition
  – face-to-face and aggressively?	

• Have you ever suspended a player for misconduct?	
• Have you ever manipulated the rules of a competition?	
• Have you ever shouted at a player for poor performance?	
• Have you ever ignored a parent who is shouting at their child?	
• Have you ever wished parents would stop attending competitions?	

It's a tough list, yet all of these are tests of character for coaches and players. Of course, the list could go on. Sport has, in the past, been accused of racism, unfairness and cheating. In fact, as you read this resource, there will no doubt be a story somewhere of a banned or disgraced participant.

So, how can we begin to develop character in our participants? A gradual development has been suggested within the 5Cs framework.

Table 12: The phased development of character and caring in the 5Cs for coaching

Stage	Young participants should:
Active Start	• understand simple rules for activities and begin to develop their own rules
FUNdamentals	• understand simple rules for specific activities and develop their own criteria for judging performance • begin to understand fair play and why cheating harms activity
Learning to Play and Practice	• show respect for the club, coaches and fellow players • understand rules of activities and follow them • follow codes of conduct.

Understanding Simple Rules for Activities and Beginning to Develop their Own Rules

As young participants begin to play, they also begin to learn sport has a structure. Learning simple rules and devising their own begins to reinforce the idea sport has a code by which to play.

Understanding Simple Rules for Specific Activities and Developing their Own Criteria for Judging Performance

As their capability improves, young participants will begin to learn rules for performance. The Key Steps award scheme run by British Gymnastics is a good example, as it gives specific criteria for performance and, if young participants reach an acceptable standard, they gain an award. Learning specific rules, such as when a free-kick is awarded or how to touch the end of a swimming pool in a turn, are also important. These examples could be even more valuable if coaches asked appropriate questions, such as: 'what would you do if you disagreed with the decision?' A useful discussion could follow where coaches could help players understand the negative effects of dwelling on decisions, or showing too much emotion in such circumstances.

Showing Respect for the Club, Coaches and Fellow Players

The sports coach UK *Code of Practice for Sports Coaches* (see Appendix 3) offers some useful ideas as to the role coaches have to play in establishing the right atmosphere for the development of character.

Table 13: Reflective activity 3

Do You...	Yes or No?	Ideas

• work with players to develop a code of conduct or practice		• The code could include:
		  – punctuality
		  – what to do if you cannot attend
		  – dress and equipment
		  – attitude

• encourage players to talk with each other and evaluate performance at the end of each session		• Spend 5–10 minutes at the end of each session with pairs or small groups of players • Talk with players about the importance of positive and constructive feedback
• encourage players to thank the coaching staff after each session		• After the evaluation, establish a routine of staying behind so players can say thank you
• expect players to put out, and clear away, equipment		• Why not establish a rota?
• talk with players about their behaviour before a game		• You will know some players who react badly to some decisions: could preparation to avoid this be part of their warm-up routine?
• encourage players to shake hands even after informal games in practice sessions		• Why not establish the routine, or ask them to suggest/develop their own (eg high fives or fist bumps)?
• have a disciplinary system for unfair play		• Could a green, yellow or red card system be used for behaviour and unfair play? • Could you ask participants to officiate themselves under appropriate supervision/guidance?
• bring in a qualified official for some practice sessions and encourage players to discuss the reasons for decisions after the game?		• This could be good practice for an older teenager, but it would need controlled supervision.

Following Codes of Conduct

As young participants develop, clubs and coaches should have a code of conduct with which they should comply. The codes of conduct below have been developed by YST.

YST Sportsmanship - Key Points

- Enjoy yourself and promote enjoyment to others
- Be responsible for your actions
- Take pride in your performance
- Encourage others to do their best
- Be a good role model
- Enjoy participating
- Practise sportsmanship in all situations.

YST - Expectations of Participants

- Treat competition as a game, not a war
- Accept all decisions by officials
- Recognise outstanding performances by opponents
- Demonstrate concern for an injured player, regardless of team
- Encourage participants to display only sportsmanlike conduct
- Shake hands with officials and fellow participants at the end of a competition, regardless of outcome
- At the end of the game, applaud performances of all participants.

Many governing bodies of sport have sample codes of conduct. Some have specific initiatives, like the 'Respect' campaign run by the Rugby Football League and 'Kicking Racism Out of Football' developed by The FA. There is a useful section on behaviour policies and codes on pages 8–11 of *Positive Behaviour Management in Sport* (Fuller et al, 2009).

SECTION SEVEN
Creativity

Definitions of **creativity** for the 5Cs for coaching have, so far, included independent thinking as well as finding new solutions to problems.

Creativity has been defined as enabling and encouraging participants to find their own solutions to problems, so they learn to understand, rather than simply copy and repeat. The following table gives some useful examples.

Table 14: Encouraging creativity in early stages of development

Stage	Young participants should:
Active Start	• be allowed to experience equipment and movement with guidance that encourages experimentation (eg moving to stories and music, playing outside on apparatus)
FUNdamentals	• be allowed to experiment in all practical situations, as well as continue to play freely as much as possible
Learning to Play and Practice	• make up their own practices and sequences • be involved in devising practices with the coach/teacher.

The easiest way to consider this type of problem solving is to enable participants to react appropriately to the 'if, then, do' cycle (see Figure 5).

This type of problem solving is crucial for all participants, especially when transferring skills from practice to competition. How many times have coaches said: 'that's not what I told them to do in practice!'

So, how is this type of creativity encouraged and established? Overleaf are some ideas.

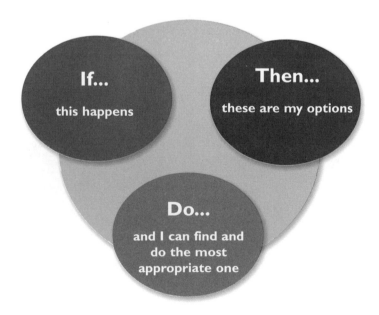

Figure 5: The 'if, then, do' cycle

Teaching Games for Understanding (TGfU)

One of the most influential models for encouraging independent thinking in games has been the TGfU model. Bunker and Thorpe (1982) believed players were more likely to transfer skills from the training ground to competition if they had been in game-like situations in practice.

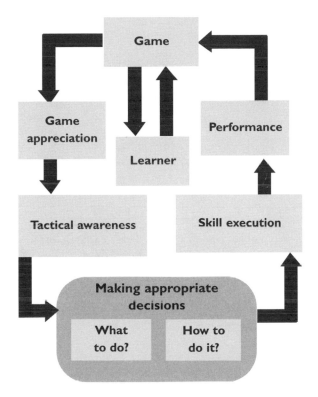

Figure 6: The Teaching Games for Understanding model (Bunker and Thorpe, 1982)

As you can see, the learner is at the centre of the TGfU model. We can all appreciate games take place in a dynamic and complicated environment of changing time, position, possession and space. In TGfU, coaches devise games with various conditions that focus on a certain principle of play. Players are then able to play in these conditions and come up with their own solutions to problems the game presents; it's a condition of almost continuous creativity.

A good example of TGfU is the three-hoop ball game, developed by Thorpe and Tan (2002). This is a simple invasion game suitable, with adaptation, for football, netball, hockey, handball, water polo, etc. The game uses six goals (rather than two) placed on the goal lines, with a goal in each corner and one in the middle. Players are

faced with a range of decisions focusing on using width and changing the direction of play. The types of creativity players can show are indicated in the following list of questions from the TOPs sport card of three-hoop ball.

Can children:

- play near one goal and then suddenly switch play to another

- keep one player behind the others, for players to move the ball from one side to the other

- discuss how to defend the hoops, but also be ready to attack as well

- discuss if one hoop is easier to score in than another

- describe why some teams defend the hoops better than others

- describe why some teams score more goals than others

- invent a practice to help with this game?

Rule and Game Making

The last question from the TOPs sport card leads on to another aspect of creativity: rule and game making. David Morley (Bailey and Morley, 2006) has used creativity as one of the multi-abilities developed for YST. In a game called square ball, Morley uses game and rule changing to enhance creative thinking in young participants. Square ball is played with four benches turned on to their side, making a square shape (see below). Teams of four squat behind the benches and each player has a number 1–4. When the coach calls a number, the player with that number from each of the four teams comes into the area and tries to score a goal, by rolling a ball on the ground to hit one of the other benches.

Players are asked to be creative with rule changes, tactics and game modifications, in a way that will enhance the strengths of the team. They are then asked to implement their ideas in the games, and analyse and evaluate their effectiveness by asking:

* why do the ideas work or not work

* did they enhance the team's success?

Reproduced with kind permission from YST's TOPs Resource Pack

Scenarios

Another idea used is the creation of scenarios to which participants can respond creatively. Below are some examples.

> * You have had two 'no jumps' in a competition. How should you prepare for the next one?
>
> * Your team is winning 25–20 in a rugby union game with five minutes to play. You have possession in the opponents' half. What should you do?
>
> * You cannot find a control in an orienteering competition. What should you do?
>
> * Your team is winning 78–76 in a basketball game and you have possession from the end line. What should you do?

Enabling players to find their own solutions to these kinds of problems gives coaches a dilemma. The coach will know what is best to do, but the players will do what they can do. Which of these is more likely to dominate in a pressurised situation?

Composition

Dancers, gymnasts, synchronised swimmers and cheerleaders are all involved in performing routines from a very early age. They can, of course, also be involved in creating them. Coaches will be aware of the ability of participants to add to routines and to find innovative ways of changing them, but the idea can also be extended to games and other areas.

When coaches plan set plays and routines, they are involved in composition. Young participants can be involved in just the same way as young gymnasts and dancers.

As a coach, you may be able to use the following scenarios.

- When the ball goes out of play, ask one team member to get together with two or more teammates to plan what they are going to do. A signal to let everyone know what is going on, apart from the opposition, should be devised.

- In striking and fielding games, ask the bowler or pitcher to plan for delivery to a certain player and then attempt it.

- In orienteering, ask one group to lay out the controls for others, making one very difficult control.

- In swimming or athletics, ask relay teams to try out different people on different legs of the relay and find out how it goes. Or, ask them to swim/run at a different pace during training to see how it feels.

These are all examples of helping participants be creative and involved in a different way during their coaching sessions.

Goal Setting

Clive Brewer lists goal setting as one of the appropriate activities for young participants at the Learning to Play and Practice stage (see Table 8 on page 12). If approached correctly, goal setting can give young participants the opportunity to be creative in their own training. Young participants could be encouraged to set innovative goals from this early stage, with coaches asking the following questions:

- How do you think you could improve on...? How much better would you like to be in three months' time?

- How much practice could you do on your own? Where could you do it safely?

- Can you read about this and tell me how we could practise it?

SECTION EIGHT
Fitting It All Together

By this stage, it is hoped you will recognise the value of the 5Cs for coaching. To help with planning, three tables have been compiled in Appendix 1 to show the interaction of the 5Cs with the physical, mental, technical and tactical development of players. You may consider it worthwhile to adopt a new type of session plan, like the one given below.

Venue:		Date:		
Duration:		Time:		
		Equipment:		
Learning from previous sessions to be applied in this session:				
Goals for the session (technical and for using the 5Cs):				
Content		**Organisation**	**Time**	**Review**
Introduction/warm-up:				
Main content (including developing competence):				
Confidence:				
Connection:				
Character and Caring:				
Creativity:				
Summary:				
Cool-down:				
Comments on the session:				

You will notice the session planner includes some new sections on the 5Cs, with competence included within the main content. Examples of how to include the 5Cs in this type of session planner for different sports are given below.

Handball

5Cs for Coaching	To Be Included This Session?	How?
Competence		Multi-skills agility game involving jumping
Confidence		
Connection		Competition at the end with chosen captains and coaches from participants
Character and Caring		Fair play talk before the competition and a simple gold card shown for demonstrations of fair play.
Creativity		

Gymnastics

5Cs for Coaching	To Be Included This Session?	How?
Competence		Coordination game involving balls and hoops as preparation for rhythmic session
Confidence		
Connection		Participants asked to judge each others' performance, along with the coach
Character and Caring		
Creativity		Participants asked to suggest an alternative move for the sequences they are judging.

Orienteering

5Cs for Coaching	To Be Included This Session?	How?
Competence		Agility session involving fast movement through semi-difficult terrain
Confidence		Selected young participants given extra help with map reading
Connection		
Character and Caring		Working in pairs and helping each other
Creativity		Particular praise given for innovative routes taken, or for good planning.

SECTION NINE
...There's One Last C!

When Lerner (2000) started work on the 5Cs model, two important connections were made.

Firstly, that promoting, encouraging and facilitating positive youth development would serve to reduce the need to invest in efforts aimed at reducing problem behaviour (this alone is quite a claim for the 5Cs, that as coaches we know we are helping young participants develop positively).

The second connection concerns young participants being helped to develop using the 5Cs, meaning they become highly likely to make a **contribution** (the final C!).

Contribution is, of course, prevalent throughout sport. Despite the fact there are many volunteers and an altogether huge workforce, there never seems to be enough people. Lack of capacity to welcome more young participants into sport is a genuine concern for our schools and clubs; more young participants developing into adults and making a contribution would be wonderful.

The following profile is of Rehana Khalil. Rehana plays professional basketball and this story illustrates her marvellous contribution to her sport. She attended Whalley Range High in Manchester and completed her first degree two years ago. Rehana is now starting a Masters. She has represented Great Britain at under-20 level and forms part of the 25-strong training squad for the women's team.

Sport has always been important to me, but, from 14 years old, it was a major decider in the way I would turn out. At school, I played all sports, but finally had to pick between netball and basketball. I chose basketball because I felt it gave me more opportunities.

There were always after-school clubs and lunch clubs, which were great as they were something to do other than schoolwork. I wasn't really keen on studies, so sport kind of gave me direction and kept me out of trouble at school.

When I began to play basketball for a club, it started off as something to do in the evenings, because it was always go to school, come home, do homework and watch TV. I wanted more meaning to being a teenager, especially coming from my culture.

As I became more involved in basketball, I became more independent: using public transport across Manchester to and from practices and matches; managing my time better; and fitting in schoolwork and basketball training.

More involvement meant having to pay for training sessions. Having to referee on a Saturday morning to make money eventually led to being a court supervisor. I got better at using my own initiative, learnt to deal with my parents in certain situations, and improved my interaction with colleagues. I really love working with other coaches, getting to know them and learning from them.

Through playing, I was able to get my coaching and refereeing qualifications. These helped with my confidence and communication with others. Before starting university, I coached basketball in schools, interacting with all age groups, teachers and parents. It gives me a good feeling that I've done something to get young people involved and I really hope they take it up.

I got a chance to play for the English Universities basketball team. I made friends from different universities while on the team and learnt more about time management. Being disciplined while studying, and finding the balance and putting in the hours to achieve the best in both basketball and study, was really important.

Basketball takes up a lot of time, so socialising outside of the sport is difficult. Over the years, I've become better at dividing my time between family, friends and basketball. Sport really teaches you about time management, although I've not quite mastered it yet!

I recently had the chance to go abroad and play as a professional. I have met more new people, experienced a whole new culture, and had the opportunity to learn a new language.

Being involved in basketball in every aspect has really made me the person I am: my character and personality has really come out. Sport has always been something real and I can call it my own. I decide how far I want to take it, how hard I'm willing to work for it, and when I'm ready to give it up.

APPENDIX 1A
The 5Cs for Coaching – Physical, Mental, Technical and Tactical Matrix for Active Start

Young participants should:

	Competence	Confidence	Connection	Character and Caring	Creativity
Physical	• adopt appropriate balance of movement activities and begin to play with objects	• be able to use progressive and positive development of movement activities in a positive and stimulating environment	• work cooperatively with others	• learn how activities can be structured (eg size of targets and number of tries)	• explore problems in a true play environment
Mental	• be able to track the movement of someone else and respond to them	• be happy with what they are doing	• explore cooperatively with others	• respond appropriately to more structured sessions	• be encouraged to adopt imaginative play
Technical	• adopt appropriate development of movement and coordination activities	• aim for an 80–100% success rate in most activities • seek guidance on emerging technique to ensure success	• begin to play with others	• show persistence	• be encouraged to play with equipment
Tactical	• be able to use space and observe its boundaries	• be able to work with others in a space and enjoy it	• begin to understand the role of others	• understand scenarios and interact with them	• understand the structure of an activity and find ways to undertake it effectively.

Young participants should:	Competence	Confidence	Connection	Character and Caring	Creativity
Physical	• adopt appropriate balance of ABCs in a multi-activity environment	• be able to use progressive and positive development of ABC activities in a positive and stimulating environment	• work cooperatively with others in larger groups (eg 3 v 1, 4 v 2, 3 v 3 and 4 v 4)	• learn how activities can be structured (eg size of targets and number of tries)	• be capable of indicating different ways of moving, according to the physical task
Mental	• be able to track an object when someone else is playing with it, or be able to track the movement of another participant	• talk about their successes	• understand individual and team performance and differentiate between the two	• respond appropriately to more structured sessions • begin to understand fair play	• plan simple and imaginative activities
Technical	• adopt appropriate development of ABCs and begin to use equipment from specific sports • be able to use both sides of the body	• aim for an 80–100% success rate in most activities • seek guidance on emerging technique to ensure success	• be capable of working with a partner on a task	• show persistence	• start to play different shots, make different moves, and be capable of simple composition
Tactical	• understand space and how to use it	• be able to work with others in a space and enjoy it	• be able to work in a space with two or three others in possession • understand different pace	• understand scenarios and interact with them	• be able to solve problems involving space, time and possession.

APPENDIX 1C
The 5Cs for Coaching – Physical, Mental, Technical and Tactical Matrix for Learning to Play and Practice

Young participants should:

	Competence	Confidence	Connection	Character and Caring	Creativity
Physical	• have more influence over sport-specific skills and practices	• begin to discuss the quality of a performance	• work cooperatively with others in larger groups (eg 5 v 3, 6 v 4, 4 v 4 5 v 5, and even 7 v 7 for the more able)	• be able to explain the benefits of practice	• be able to offer a range of solutions to any physical task
Mental	• be able to combine basic skills efficiently • be able to cope with different environments	• understand and be able to use positive self-talk	• understand individual and team performance and differentiate between the two	• begin to understand fair play and comment where others have not played to the rules	• be able to set simple goals and involve others in achieving them
Technical	• possess the ability to use speed and strength appropriately • be able to develop endurance	• aim for an 80–100% success rate in most activities and a 100% success rate in basic activities	• be able to organise a task for a small group	• be able to practise something for a longer period of time	• be able to explain the composition for others • be able to respond to different challenges from others in an activity
Tactical	• be able to match technical ability with tactical problems	• be able to experiment with different solutions by trial and error, and be able to accept things that go wrong, in a positive way	• be able to talk about how to do an activity in a way to gain advantage within the rules and spirit of the activity	• be able to cope with modified sports with modified rules, and understand how the rules positively shape the activity	• be able to devise a game plan • be able to plan a performance and differentiate when peak performance is required.

APPENDIX 2
Blank Session Planner

Venue:	Date:
Duration:	Time:
	Equipment:

Learning from previous sessions to be applied in this session:

Goals for the session:

Content	Organisation	Time	Review
Introduction/warm-up:			
Main content (including developing competence):			
Confidence:			
Connection:			
Character and Caring:			
Creativity:			
Summary:			
Cool-down:			

Comments on the session:

Code of Practice for Sports Coaches

Rights/Relationships/Responsibilities

sports coach
UK
The National Coaching Foundation

Great Coaches...Great Sport

Code of Practice for Sports Coaches

Coaches play a crucial role in the development of any sport and in the lives of the performers they coach. Good coaches ensure participants in sport have positive experiences and are therefore more likely to continue in their sport and achieve their potential.

Coaching, as an emerging profession, must demonstrate a high degree of honesty, integrity and competence at all levels. The need for coaches to understand and act upon their responsibilities is of critical importance to sport, as is the need to protect the key concept of participation for fun and enjoyment as well as achievement. This is implicit within good coaching practice and promotes a professional image of the good practitioner. This Code of Practice defines all that is best in good coaching practice.

Good coaching practice needs to reflect the following key principles:

- ### Rights

  Coaches must respect and champion the rights of every individual to participate in sport.

- ### Relationships

  Coaches must develop a relationship with performers (and others) based on openness, honesty, mutual trust and respect.

- ### Responsibilities – personal standards

  Coaches must demonstrate proper personal behaviour and conduct at all times.

- ### Responsibilities – professional standards

  To maximise the benefits and minimise the risks to performers, coaches must attain a high level of competence through qualifications, and a commitment to ongoing training that ensures safe and correct practice.

  These principles are defined in more detail further in this brochure.

Code of Practice for Sports Coaches

Principle	Statement	Issues	Actions
Rights	Coaches must respect and champion the rights of every individual to participate in sport	Coaches should: • assist in the creation of an environment where every individual has the opportunity to participate in a sport or activity of their choice • create and maintain an environment free of fear and harassment • recognise the rights of all performers to be treated as individuals • recognise the rights of performers to confer with other coaches and experts • promote the concept of a balanced lifestyle, supporting the well-being of the performer both in and out of the sport.	• Treat all individuals in sport with respect at all times. • Do not discriminate on the grounds of gender, marital status, race, colour, disability, sexual identity, age, occupation, religious beliefs or political opinion. • Do not condone or allow any form of discrimination to go unchallenged. • Do not publicly criticise or engage in demeaning descriptions of others. • Be discreet in any conversations about performers, coaches or any other individuals. • Communicate with and provide feedback to performers in a manner that reflects respect and care.

Principle	Statement	Issues	Actions
Relationships	Coaches must develop a relationship with performers (and others) based on openness, honesty, mutual trust and respect	Coaches: • must not engage in behaviour that constitutes any form of abuse (physical, sexual, emotional, neglect, bullying) • should promote the welfare and best interests of their performers • must avoid sexual intimacy with performers either while coaching them or in the period of time immediately following the end of the coaching relationship • must take action if they have a concern about the behaviour of an adult towards a child • should empower performers to be responsible for their own decisions • should clarify the nature of the coaching services being offered to performers • should communicate and cooperate with other organisations and individuals in the best interests of performers.	• Be aware of the physical needs of performers, especially the developmental stage and needs of children and young people, and ensure that training loads and intensities are appropriate. • Ensure that physical contact is appropriate and necessary, and is carried out within recommended guidelines (provided by governing bodies of sport) with the performer's full consent and approval. • Do not engage in any form of sexually related contact with any performer for whom they have responsibility. This is strictly forbidden as is sexual innuendo, flirting or inappropriate gestures and terms. Coaches are in a position of power and trust in relation to performers. By entering into an intimate/sexual relationship with a performer, a coach may be deemed guilty of abusing this position and, in relation to children and young people, this may also be unlawful. • Inform parents or guardians immediately if you are at all concerned about the welfare of a child, unless there are concerns that this would not be in the interests of the child. • Know and understand the relevant governing body of sport or employer child protection/safeguarding policies and procedures in this regard and adhere to them. • Follow the reporting procedures laid down by your governing body of sport or employer if you have a concern – non-action is unacceptable. • Arrange to transfer a performer to another coach if it is clear that an inappropriate or intimate relationship is developing. • Discuss with parents and other interested parties the potential impact of the programme on the performer. • Respect performers' opinions when making decisions about their participation in their sport. • Encourage performers to take responsibility for their own development and actions. • Allow performers to discuss and participate in the decision-making process. • Discuss and agree with performers what information is confidential. • Inform performers or their parents/guardians of the requirements of the sport. • Inform performers or their parents/guardians of any potential costs involved in accessing the coaching services on offer. • Be aware of and communicate on any conflict of interest as soon as it becomes apparent. • Do not work with any other coach's performer without first discussing or agreeing it with both the coach and the performer involved. • Identify and agree with performers which other experts or organisations could offer appropriate services.

Continued overleaf

Code of Practice for Sports Coaches

Principle	Statement	Issues	Actions
Responsibilities – personal standards	Coaches must demonstrate proper personal behaviour and conduct at all times	Coaches: • must be fair, honest and considerate to performers and others in their sport • should project an image of health, cleanliness and functional efficiency • must be positive role models for performers at all times.	• Operate within the rules and the spirit of your sport. • Educate performers on issues relating to the use of performance-enhancing drugs in sport and cooperate fully with UK Sport and governing bodies of sport policies. • Maintain the same level of interest and support when a performer is sick or injured. • Display high standards in use of language, manner, punctuality, preparation and presentation. • Encourage performers to display the same qualities. • Do not smoke, drink alcohol or use recreational drugs before or while coaching. This reflects a negative image and could compromise the safety of your performers. • Display control, respect, dignity and professionalism to all involved in your sport.
Principle	**Statement**	**Issues**	**Actions**
Responsibilities – professional standards	To maximise the benefits and minimise the risks to performers, coaches must attain a high level of competence through qualifications, and a commitment to ongoing training that ensures safe and correct practice	Coaches will: • ensure the environment is as safe as possible, taking into account and minimising possible risks • promote the execution of safe and correct practice • be professional and accept responsibility for their actions • make a commitment to providing a quality service to their performers • actively promote the positive benefits to society of participation in sport, including the positive contribution sport can make to achieving improved outcomes for children and young people[1] • contribute to the development of coaching as a profession by exchanging knowledge and ideas with others, and by working in partnership with other agencies and professionals • gain governing bodies of sport coaching qualifications appropriate to the level at which they coach.	• Follow the guidelines of your governing body of sport or employer. • Plan all sessions so they meet the needs of the performers and are progressive and appropriate. • Maintain appropriate records of your performers. • Recognise and accept when it is appropriate to refer a performer to another coach or specialist. • Seek to achieve the highest level of qualification available. • Demonstrate commitment to Continuing Professional Development (CPD) by undertaking/attending learning opportunities to maintain up-to-date knowledge of technical developments in your sport. • Undertake/attend CPD opportunities to maintain up-to-date knowledge and understanding of other issues that might impact on both you and your performers. • Be aware of the social issues and how your sport can contribute to local, regional or national initiatives. • Actively participate in recruitment and education opportunities in your sport. • Actively contribute to local, regional and national initiatives to improve the standards and quality of coaching both in your sport and sport in general. • Practise in an open and transparent fashion that encourages other coaches to contribute to or learn from your knowledge and experience. • Engage in self-analysis and reflection to identify your professional needs. • Seek CPD opportunities to develop your coaching skills and competencies, and update your knowledge. • Manage your lifestyle and coaching commitments to avoid burnout that might impair your performance. • Do not assume responsibility for any role for which you are not qualified or prepared. • Do not misrepresent your level of qualification. • Promote good coaching practice in others and challenge any poor practice that you become aware of.

[1] www.everychildmatters.gov.uk

Implementation Issues

It is recognised and identified by the Ethics Review Group that a code of practice in isolation is of minimal value. In order for this code to fully impact on coaching practice and behaviour, it must:

- be incorporated into governing bodies of sport or employer constitutions and governance documents
- be a constituent part of a policy and procedure for dealing with allegations and complaints
- be used as the definitive guide and benchmark measure of coaching practice in determining any need for sanctions against a coach
- be fully incorporated into the coach education processes
- be assessed as part of the coach accreditation process
- be supported by the appropriate training and resources.

sports coach UK has developed a suite of training resources that underpin many of the concepts contained within this Code of Practice for Sports Coaches.

These are:

- *Safeguarding and Protecting Children* (formerly *Good Practice and Child Protection*)
- *Equity in Your Coaching*
- *The Responsible Sports Coach*
- *Coaching and the Law.*

This Code of Practice, developed by sports coach UK, provides a guide for good and safe coaching practice.

sports coach UK will support a governing body of sport in implementing this code of practice.

sports coach UK will ensure that it has professional and ethical values and that all its practices are inclusive and equitable.

sports coach UK
114 Cardigan Road
Headingley
Leeds LS6 3BJ
Tel: 0113-274 4802
Fax: 0113-275 5019
Email: coaching@sportscoachuk.org
Website: www.sportscoachuk.org

References and Further Reading

Bailey, R. and Morley, D. (2006) *Meeting the Needs of Your Most Able Pupils: Physical Education and Sport.* London: David Fulton Publishers. ISBN: 978-1-843123-34-7.

Bunker, D. and Thorpe, R. (1982) 'A model for the teaching of games in the secondary school', *Bulletin of Physical Education,* 10: 9–16.

Campbell, S. and Crisfield, P. (2008) *Making Sport Fun.* Leeds: Coachwise Business Solutions. ISBN: 978-1-902523-81-4.

Côté, J., Bruner, M., Strachan, L., Erickson, K. and Fraser-Thomas, J. (in press) 'Athletes development and coaching', in Lyle, J. and Cushion, C. *Sport Coaching: Professionalism and Practice.* Oxford: Elsevier.

Côté, J. (2007) 'Opportunities and pathways for beginners to elite to ensure optimum and lifelong involvement in sport', *Junior Sport Matters: Briefing Papers for Australian Junior Sport.* Australian Sports Commission.

Côté, J. and Gilbert, W. (2009) 'An integrative definition of coaching effectiveness and expertise', *International Journal of Sports Science and Coaching,* 4 (3).

Foreman, G. and Bradshaw, A. (2009) *An Introduction to the FUNdamentals of Movement.* Leeds: Coachwise Business Solutions. ISBN: 978-1-905540-70-9.

Fuller, N., Chapman, J. and Jolly, S. (2009) *Positive Behaviour Management in Sport.* Leeds: Coachwise Business Solutions. ISBN: 978-1-905540-58-7.

Gordon, R. and Joyce, G. (2009) *Safeguarding and Protecting Children 2: Reflecting on Practice.* Leeds: Coachwise Business Solutions. ISBN: 978-1-905540-73-0.

Hagger, M. and Biddle, S. (2008) *Coaching Young Performers.* Leeds: Coachwise Business Solutions. ISBN: 978-1-902523-56-3.

Haskins, D. (2008) 'Developing the coaches of tomorrow', *coaching edge* 13: 12–13.

Haskins, D. (2008) 'Optimising training for young people', *coaching edge* 12: 12–13.

Jelicic, H., Bobek, D. L., Phelps, E., Lerner R. M. and Lerner, J. V. (2007) 'Using positive youth development to predict contribution and risk behaviours in early adolescence – findings from the first two waves of the 4-H study of positive youth development', *International Journal of Behavioural Development,* 31 (3): 263–273.

Lerner, R. M. (2005) *Promoting Positive Youth Development: Theoretical and Empirical Bases.* Washington: National Research Council/Institute of Medicine, National Academies of Science.

Lerner, R. M., Fisher, C. B and Weinberg, R. A. (2000) 'Toward a science for and of the people: promoting civil society through the application of developmental science', *Child Development,* 71, 11–20.

Roth, J. L. and Brooks-Gunn, J. (2003) 'What exactly is a youth development programme? Answers from research and practice', *Applied Developmental Science,* (7): 94–111.

Stafford, I. (2005) *Coaching for Long-term Athlete Development.* Leeds: Coachwise Business Solutions. ISBN: 978-1-902523-70-9.

The National Coaching Foundation (2009) *An Introduction to the FUNdamentals of Movement* (DVD).

The National Coaching Foundation (2009) *FUNdamentals of Agility* (DVD).

The National Coaching Foundation (2009) *FUNdamentals of Balance* (DVD).

The National Coaching Foundation (2009) *FUNdamentals of Coordination* (DVD).

Thorpe, R. and Tan, S. (2002) *TOP Sport Invasion Games.* Loughborough: Youth Sport Trust.

Youth Sport Trust (2003) *TOPs Gymnastics.* Loughborough: Youth Sport Trust.

Youth Sport Trust (2007) *Girls Active: An Inspirational Resource Pack.* Loughborough: Youth Sport Trust.